THE LAST POETS
VIBES FROM THE SCRIBES
Selected Poems

THE LAST POETS

Selected Poems

VIBES FROM THE SCRIBES

Africa World Press, Inc.

P.O. Box 1892
Trenton, New Jersey 08607

Africa World Press, Inc.
P.O. Box 1892
Trenton NJ 08607

First Africa World Press Edition 1992

Cover Design by Paul Tucker, Jr.

Library of Congress Catalog Card Number: 91-78312

ISBN: 0-86543-316-X Cloth
         0-86543-317-8 Paper

CONTENTS

INTRODUCTION

Of all the lines included in this collection – a collection which spans almost 20 years, from the late 1960s to the mid-1980s – the one that for me most tellingly sums up The Last Poets comes from the chorus to Suliaman El Hadi's *Blessed Are Those Who Struggle*: 'Better to die for a noble cause than to live and die a slave'.

A recurring theme in the Poets' work is expressed in the celebratory *Ho Chi Minh*, where the frail guerilla leader warns the all-powerful American invader: 'Before we would submit, you see, we all would rather die'. The sentiment encapsulates both the political thrust of the Poets' work and the economic reality of the group members' actual lives.

For the Poets there is a wafer-thin dividing line between their personal life and their recorded work, and there lies the reason for much of the impact and relevance of the latter. Fêted by the white liberal media all over the English-speaking world for over 15 years (ever since the release of their first album, 'The Last Poets', in 1970), the Poets today continue to live in the same economically deprived conditions where they first took to the Harlem street corners to recite poetry in the late '60s. Unusually among the 'protest artists' who emerged in America during the '60s, the poets really *were* members of the class they championed, and occasionally vilified, in their work. They weren't merely identifying with dispossessed urban

American blacks; they *were* these people. And since then, despite the massive media acclaim, they have remained these people – partly from choice, partly because white ethnocentric America does not reward real revolutionaries with honorary professorships and the like. Had they recanted, the individual Poets would doubtless be making a fat living on the college lecture circuit.

Reading these poems up to 15 years after they were first recorded is still an intense experience. Born in the ephemeral worlds of the street corner and the popular record, their passion, anger, wit, irony and style have survived entirely unscathed. On the one hand, this is a testament to the sheer literary skill of Jalal Nuriddin and Suliaman El Hadi; on the other it is a chilling reflection of how little white America has managed – or even tried – in the 1970s and 1980s to right the wrongs and disadvantages it has inflicted on its black people. The racial tensions and injustices mapped out so vividly on early works like *On the Subway* or *White Man's Got A God Complex* (from 'The Last Poets', 1970, and 'This Is Madness, 1971, respectively) are still very much a part of the black experience today. So too are the feelings of inferiority and impotence among black people which inspired the vitriolic *Wake Up Niggers* and *Niggers Are Scared Of Revolution* from their 1970 debut.

Remarkably, in the light of unjust social conditions and unchangingly grim personal economic life, the Poets themselves have changed and grown over the last 15 years, most notably in their racial attitudes. Coming together as young men in the ugly confluence of the New York ghetto hustle in the late '60s – a world of poverty, crime, prison, hard drugs and alcohol – they turned first to the separatist Black Muslim philosophy espoused by the late Elijah Muhammad. But, like Malcolm X, another Black Muslim refugee from the hustling life, the Poets grew to realize that Elijah Muhammad's anti-white beliefs ran counter to the true meaning of Islam, a religion which, despite its shortcomings (which in the West are most strongly perceived in its attitudes to women), actively propagates the equality of all races. While the Poets today are as pro-black as they ever were, they are every bit as fervently pro-white, pro-yellow . . . pro-human. So those poems from their 1985 album 'Oh My People' included here are directed as much at white people as they are at black: *This Is Your Life* is a warning of an impending nuclear armageddon which will make no racial exceptions. *Get Movin'* and the poem *Oh My People* itself can be taken as being directed at black people; but they can also be taken, and are intended to be taken, as 9 talking to the white working classes who share the same deprivations and feelings of powerlessness as their black brothers and sisters.

In this context, however, it is important to remember that the Last Poets were never, even in the heady Black Muslim days, exclusively concerned with racial issues – and some of their most powerful and long-lasting works, while obviously coming from a black perspective, are not directly concerned with race. *E Pluribus Unum*, for instance, one of Nuriddin's most impressively original poems, is a dissection of the symbolism behind the design of the dollar bill, and that symbolism's meaning for the American economy. Similarly El Hadi's *Delights Of The Garden* is poetry of genuinely epic proportions.

Far from exclusively black in outlook are the anti-drug *Jones Coming Down* and *O.D.* Both of them early works, at the time they were written the heroin plague had long since spread from black ghettos to white suburbs. *Jazzoetry* and *Bird's Word* too, though celebrating the black creators of jazz music, do not simultaneously set out to belittle white contributions.

'Politics,' Nuriddin observed while discussing these poems with me in early 1985, 'is no longer a skin issue. There are bigger issues facing us now, that black and white must overcome together – or we will perish together.'

Chris May, August 1985

POEMS BY JALAL NURIDDIN

A black man and a white man are riding the subway together. The black man notices that the white man is staring at him. They get into a staredown. It gets into a psych thing, no-one blinking but each one thinking. Both wondering what's on the other's mind. Each one seeing, the blind side of mind. Finally the white man blinks and the black man thinks: You are guilty of hate. But the feeling has become mutual. Guilt manifesting into hate, and frustration manifesting into hate. Finally his stop comes up, and he leaves abrupt, thinking with pride, his eyes have not lied. In this complex quiz, he is heartened to know who he is. And so he heads for home in Neo-Rome, alienated and alone in the heart of the ghetto, his own Sow-Etto.

On the sub**wayyy**yyyyyy
I dug the man digging on me
But the dude was hung up in a **mass** of confusion as to who I was
He thought **he** was trying to see
But you see, but you see
Me knowing me
Black, proud and determined to be free
Could plainly see my enemy yes, yes

                            Yes I know him

I once slaved for him body and soul
and made him a pile of black gold
off the sweat of my labour he stole
But his game, his game is old
we've broken the mental hold
Things must change
There's no limit to our range
He can never understand
the new black man
less lone see us every day
riding the sub**wayyy**yyy

             8th Avenue 7th Avenue 6th Avenue

                     IND BMT IRT

14   He **still** hasn't dug me
He stares endlessly
Blinking
          blink blink, blink blink,
                    blink blink, blink blink,
                              blink blink, blink blink,
                                        blink blink, blink blink,
                                                  He's on the brink
about to sink
I ask you
Shall I save him? Can he be saved?

No! No! No!

Next stop 125th Street!

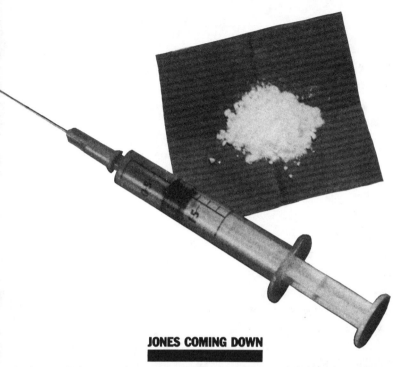

JONES COMING DOWN

It is a well-known documented fact that drug addiction is at plague proportions in the US and has been for at least three decades now. 'Jones Coming Down' is a testimony to the animal-level life of a dope addict. Unable to cope with the stark reality of everyday existence in the ghetto, the dope addict seeks to escape from his/her miserable existence in the day to day struggle to survive. In 'Jones Coming Down' we see the unrelenting compulsion of the drug addict to acquire drugs by any means necessary. 'Jones', a euphemism for habit, also known as 'monkey on my back', is a compelling force, so strong that the drug addict cannot resist it even though he or she may want to. All of the physical symptoms of withdrawal are told in this tale. The 'Junky' must cop (purchase) these drugs at all cost, even if it means risking his or her life. Drug importation in the US has not arisen by accident and is a multi-billion dollar business annually. Ignored by the federal authorities, when it was first introduced in the black communities in America, it has now spread to the white communities as well as all walks of life. As long as fantasy is perpetuated as reality, drug addiction will continue unabated, and the drug addict will continue to seek refuge in the fantasies of his or her realities.

Day breaks
Got the shakes
nose runnin'
Joint drippin'
mind slippin'
Body aches
Jones comin' down
Got an attitude
Fightin' mad
Feelin' bad
Funeral sad
Another twenty four hour drag
Jim, I need me some **scag**
Pawn my brother's do rag
to cop me a transparent thin bag
Y'see, y'see, 'cause I'm

          I'm strung out, strung out on a white witch
My timeless bitch
Riding a white horse into my main vein

Damn baby! Got to kill this pain!
I'm gon' run along and get slick
and get my woman to pull a trick
She don't care, she's on welfare
Gonna steal her check and cop me a deck
and deal me some stuff when the goin' gets rough
Where's my **wine?** I've got to ease my mind
Is that the kid I hear cryin'?
Shut up, kid! You want the super to call the man
and have me pull another bid?
So what if you're hungry!
Shit! My **Jones** is down on me!
I ain't your old man
I don't know where the dude is
If he knows what I know, he's out getting his

Damn! This pain is gettin' worse
Let me see how much dough this whore got in her purse
Well now, six dollars will cop me two small trays
and that's enough to take my gorilla Jones away.
Now let me see what's happenin' on the corner today
Hey there's my man, brother sweet stuff Sam
Hey Sam, can I get a play on a double tray
so I can take off and lay
Okay woman get up out of bed
you heard what I said
I'm a tie a rope around my arm and heat the cooker
and I want you to get your ass out on the corner
and play hooker
Wow! I can feel it now
this stuff is boss
I can see that whore on that horse
Hey **ba-by!**
Wait for **me!**
'cause I'm gon' be
Free! Free! Free! Free! Freeeeeeeee!

Really?

My horn, born interpretation of saying what the musicians are playing. Metaphysical arrangements, musical estrangements, melodious derangements is the story of jazzoetry. Taking the word jazz and poetry, dropping the 'p' on poetry and calling it jazzoetry. 'Transpositional' word play, link rhyme in space and time. We climb to a crescendo then swing on out. That's what jazzoetry is all about. Ideas connect, intersect, respecting, injecting, projecting accolades of thought are all brought out, in a torrential spout which hits with clout, makes you want to shout! Each line making its own intense sense. We move on, like notes out of a horn, flooding the landscape with images from scenes of musical dreams reams and reams of soft loud screams interlocking the methodology of musicology. Each word fated to be interrelated. Jazzoetry is sound poetry.

Rhythms and sounds

in leaps and bounds

Scales and notes and endless quotes

Hey! Black soul being told

Hypnotizing while improvising is mentally appetizing

Off on a tangent

Ain't got a cent

Searching, soaring, exploring,

              seek and you shall find

                      More time, more time

More time, more time

        More time, more time

              More time, more time

to find who? How? Where were you? Are you blue?

We're not thru digging the new

Climbing higher, soul's on fire

Seeking the top, can't stop, dig bop!

Left earth on a new birth

In space, out space, our place and face us.
Regenerated less complicated, vibrating, educating, stimulating
Young and old as a whole
Those who know **jazz** is prose
And how it goes and is going to be
Me, us, we, free
Baby can't you see
Hey! Check it out without a doubt what it's all about then shout!
Off and on, being born
Rhythmically in a wail can't fail, **smooth** sail
Break it down, run it around
and give it a pound on the town in the world
dig the sound of our **love** inside our pride that's on the ride
Jazzoetry is poetry!
Getting hat on a scat
The beginning of this, the end of that
Riffing on a cue, the play is never through
Solid, baby! Me and you
Smooth glowin' and flowin' while your horn is blowin'
Puttin' on the show
                    digging some mo' **black ego!**
Going up, growin' up that's us
Smokin', cooking, hard boiled like a cobra-coiled
Blowing your **mind** to rhythmic time
Digging up driving, striving, arriving at conclusions
Life and death **all** in one breath!
Minor chords, soft keys, summer breeze, winter freeze, listen **please!**
Breakin' the rules, schooling the fools
Jazz is cool that's the truth
dig my proof rhythm and swing doing your thing
Abnormally, informally, Jazzoetry is poetry
Poetic vibes, masculine bass
Flute and drums pick up the pace
Piano keys on a spiralling flight

That's jazzoetry in black and white
Brilliant colours, glowing hues
intimate expressions, personal views
Spreadin' the news, by way of the **blues**
Brothers, others, lovers, mothers, sons, friends
                                        Brothers, others, lovers,
mothers, sons, friends
                    Brothers, others, lovers, mothers, sons, friends
On the set — ain't none of y'all been freed yet!
Trying to pin what's happening
what you're coming from and going to
Communicating with me and you
internal **feeling** is spiritually healing
When I'm dealing with **jazz**
that **has** turned me on
Blow that horn!
Of course it's boss, get on your horse
And ride with pride jazz and poetry side by side!

SURRISES

'Surprises' deals with the 'double cross' aka the broken promises given to black people in America that were never kept. It promises that in end you should not be surprised at the ultimate surprise: genocide!

Night falls
and the sun rises
and I dig niggers, niggers, niggers of **all** shades and sizes
And the sun, the sun it plays on my eyes
and I hear the hungry cries
of black children
Their stomachs turned inside out
Their minds full of fear and doubt
Being told lies
Being watched by spies
with loophole proof alibis
While another nigger, nigger, nigger in Vietnam dies
But the sun still rises and the night still falls
and junkies still O.D. in ghetto halls
and Miles he still blows
and the oppression still grows
and where it stops, nobody knows
And black people cry out in vain

against injustice and pain
to one whose mind is insane
and it doesn't need to rain
for their tears have poured for years
And uncle tom, tom, tom
he watches over us and under us
and around us and through us
night in and day out
And we are loved for being ignorant
and hated if we are militant
but promises can do nothing for me
it's time to set ourselves free
But time marches on and the races grows strong
stronger than ajax
And niggers want to be free
but they still watch TV even though they can't see
And our chinese brothers don't cop no plea
for they are hip to unity
Isn't that the way we want to be?
But the man watches amused
'cause black people are confused
Conquered and divided
Tricked and undecided
and the good guys are dead
with slugs through their head
But the night still falls
and the sun still rises
and the man, the man, the man
is still full of tricky **Surprise! Niggers!**

O.D. is the abbreviation for overdose. Lost in the music to 'soothe the savage beast' our victim reels in his imagination while 'saturated' with heroin. Unable to separate his realities from his fantasies, he slips deeper and deeper into a catatonic state, not realizing that he's at the point of no return, and for him there will be no turning back. When his realities return, he's already been pronounced dead, and finds himself being buried. The sudden shock of that reality is too great to bear, and so he dies/alive.

Bird lives!

the brother wrote on the rotted pasteboard wall

right next to the sign that read

PLEASE DON'T PEE IN OUR HALL

And then he reached in his slide

and pulled out the tiny transparent bag

the one filled with the chalk white powder the junkies call *scag*

He *sighed* **as he hit the big vein in his arm**

and his mind took off on Bird's musical charm

Now Brother Bird was blowing *Embraceable You*

like only he was hip to the secret he knew

Wow! **the brother said as he slipped off into a nod**

Bird sure eases the pain

Now I wanna hear Brother **John** *Coltrane*

He tried to get up

but his body wouldn't move

His mind told him his senses were in a groove

Finally Bird was through

and 'trane took over in a spiritual debut

His heart began to pound

as he dug the boss sound

Damn! Bird and 'trane sure enough was down

And then he looked up and saw
that the box wasn't even **on**
and it was damn near dawn

I'm high!

I'm blind!

I'm wasted!

If I could only come down
There I go There I go There I go There I go There I go There I go
There I go There I go There I go There I go There I go
There I go There I go There I go There I go There I go

Shit! *Give me some* dough
so I can buy me some smack
and get back on the fast track
He slipped off into a nod
and the sounds became odd
and he could no longer hear 'trane or Bird
He could only hear the loud unspoken word
Get Back Nigger, you're black
No, but I'm beautiful he said
And then he suddenly realized that he was dead
and he was being lowered into the ground
and couldn't utter a single sound
and his family and friends were standing around
with their heads hanging down
crying and carrying on
'cause their beautiful black son was gone
No, I'm not dead
his mind said

Don't bury me
'cause I didn't

I didn't I didn't I didn't I didn't I didn't I didn't I didn't
I didn't I didn't I didn't I didn't I didn't I didn't
I didn't I didn't I didn't I didn't I didn't I didn't
I didn't I didn't I didn't I didn't I didn't
I didn't I didn't I didn't
And then he realized

O.D.

O.D.

O.D.

O.D.

Sun **up** down
on the corner **up**town
I turn around and hear the sound
of voices talking about who's gonna die next
'cause the **white** man's got a **God** complex
Silent niggers scream for help
Ahh, help me, help me
Nigger, make your own help
Shit! you need it
I turn around and hear the sound
of jukeboxes playing in bars
Pimps parked outside in big pretty Cadillac cars
cleaner than a broke dick dog
Sittin' in a big fine hog
dressed very fine in a mohair silk vine
But, Jim, they'll die next
'cause the **white** man's got a **God** complex
Hey, brother, what's your sport, my man?
I got just the thing for you
only cost ten and two
what you gon' do, baby?
I got black ones, brown ones, red ones, yellow ones
I even got a white one if you want to buy some
Yeah, that's right
Two-fifty-eight
Play it staight
I got it all worked out
I know what I'm talking about
I've been reading my dream book
Ain't no way in the world the kid gon' get took

Nigger, what you mean I didn't hit?
Nigger, you full of shit
Lick dice
Uh, now seven
Come on be nice and hit eleven
Well, what you know, it's Little Joe
Eh, my man got twenty dollars say Little Joe don't blow
Uh Ha. Baby needs a new pair of shoes
Uh Ha. Papa got the funky blues
Uh Ha. Mama plays the crossword in the News
Snake eyes! Sorry, nigger, you lose
The line forms to the rear, lady
and I don't care if you never cash your welfare checks

'cause the white man's got a God complex

But I got ten babies I ain't got no man
I ain't got no choice but to hold out my hand
and feed my young ones the best way I can
Eh! Man, what you mean no doubles on blackjack?
Punk, you better change that rule
'cause I ain't no fool
You better be cool, Jim, or you'll die next

'cause the white man's got a God complex

Eh, my man,
I wanna cop a nickel bag
You say all you got is scag?
Wow, that's a drag
'cause I don't want to cop no
Dope is death next

'cause the white man's got a God complex

Hey, baby, where's the gig at tonight?
Well, there's one over at Slick's for faggots and tricks
There's one around graveyard side of town
but that'll cost you a pound

But if you go and know what I know
you better pack your piece at least
or you'll die next

'cause the white man's got a God complex

Mr Stein, I done paid enough rent for this pad to be mine
but you just want to cheat me 'cause I ain't your kind
Damn! can't you see the place is falling down?
No, you can't dig it 'cause you ain't never around
Damn! I'm so poor
I don't know what the hell I'm a do any more
Not from this day to the next

'cause the white man's got a God complex

I'm makin' guns I'm God!

I'm makin' bombs I'm God!

I'm makin' gas I'm God!

I'm makin' freak machines I'm God!

Birth control pills I'm God!

Killed Indians who discovered him I'm God!

Killed Japanese with the A-bomb I'm God!

Killed and still killin' black people I'm God!

Enslaving the earth I'm God!

Done went to the moon I'm God! I'm God! I'm God! I'm God! I'm God! I'm God! I'm God! I'm God! I'm God! I'm God! I'm God! I'm God! I'm God!

I'm God!

TRUE BLUES

We start at the beginning of the journey from Africa to America. From the Southern cotton field to the black migration north during the late 20s, 30s, 40s and peaking during the 50s. The blues represent the raw emotion emitted from the slaves as a pure outlet for their sufferings. In each episode we see the blues evolve into its present day form. The poem ends in the blackest of blues – 'The Womb to the Tomb'. The lesson in the blues is the true news of a continuity of a gauntlet of soulful views: one worth a thousand pictures.

True blues ain't no new news
'bout who's been abused
for the blues is as old as my stolen soul
I sang the **blues** when the missionaries came
passing out Bibles in Jesus' name
I sang the **blues** in the hull of the ship
beneath the sting of the slavemaster's whip
I sang the **blues** when the ship anchored the dock
my family being sold on a slave block
I sang the **blues** being torn from my first born
and hung my head and cried
when my wife took his life and then committed suicide
I sang the **blues** on the slavemaster's plantation
helping him build his 'free' nation
I sang the **blues** in the cotton field

hustlin' to make the daily yield
I sang the **blues** when he forced my woman to bed
Lord knows! I wished he was dead
I sang the **blues** on the run
duckin' the dog and dodging the gun
I sang the **blues** hangin' from the tree
in a desperate attempt to break free
I sang the **blues** from sunup to down
cursing the master when he wasn't around
I sang the **blues** in all his wars
dying for some unknown cause
I sang the **blues** in a high tone, low moan
loud groan, soft grunt, hard funk!
I sang the **blues** on land, sea and air
about who, when, why and where
I sang the **blues** in church on Sunday
Slavin' on Monday
Misused on Tuesday
Abused on Wednesday
Accused on Thursday
Fried alive on Friday
And died on Saturday
Sho'nuff singin' the blues
I sang the **blues** in the summer, fall, winter and spring
I know sho'nuff that the blues is my thing
I sang the backwater blues
Rhythm and blues
Gospel blues
St Louis blues
Crosstown blues
Chcago blues
Mississippi Goddam blues

The Watts blues
Harlem blues
Hough blues
Gutbucket blues
Funky Junkie blues
I sang the Up North Cigarette Cough blues
The Down South Strung Out On The Side Of My Mouth blues
I sang the blues black
I sang the blues blacker
I sang the blues blackest
I sang about my sho'nuff blue blackness

In 1970 the poem 'Wake Up Niggers' was used as part of the sound track in the film 'Performance', although I never derived any financial benefit from it other than the brief notoriety from having the Last Poets' name associated with Mick Jagger. 'Wake Up Niggers' demands that Black Americans wake themselves up from the degradation and misery, despair and general hopelessness that reigns supreme in the ghettoes of America. Whether or not this happens remains to be seen. But if and when they do, you can count on 'the blood running in the streets' because it will be a rude awakening and they will be dealt with like the people of the South.

**Night descends
as the sun's light ends
and black comes to blend again
and with the death of the sun
night and blackness become one
Blackness being you
peeping through the red the white and the blue
Dreaming of boss black civilizations
that once flourished and grew**

Hey! Wake up niggers! Or y'all through!

**Drowning in a puddle of the white man's spit
as you pause for some draws in a mist of shit
and you ain't got nothin' to save your funky ass with
You cool fool
Sipping on a menthol cigarette 'round midnight
Rapping about how the Big Apple is outa sight
You ain't never had a bite
Who are you fooling?
Me? You?
Wake up niggers! Or y'all through
And uptown two roaches are drowning in each other's piss
And downtown inter-racial lovers secretly kiss
While junkies are dreaming of total bliss**

38

somewhere in the atmosphere
far away from here
beyond realms of white dimensions
gathered by suppressed intentions
as their cries, cries, cries
go unrecognized
except by their keeper
the grim reaper
Save me a corner, you shout
as the lights go out 'cause you ain't paid the electric bill
and the rats and roaches move in for the kill
as your lips struggle to drain that last drop from the wine bottle
and you roll snake-eyed
never realizing that you blew
Wake up niggers! Or y'all through!
Sitting in the corners with your minds
tied to your behinds
Bona fide members of Niggers Anonymous
Never knowing which way you're going
Pimping off life
Turning tricks for slick dicks
with candy asses

All masses to be held tomorrow morning for the late, great black man

Amen!

Do you niggers understand?
Up against the wall, black Maryland farmers
or I'll blow you away
and you'll never live to see the light of day
and the nightstick, the nightstick
it glides gracefully up side your head
That's right brothers and sisters
you the living dead

But the cock crows
and the night goes
and it saves your ass in nick of time
as you wake up and start to find
yourself laying up in bed
scratching your ass and head
trying to remember from where
when you recall this familiar nightmare
that always leaves you feeling blue
but you still can't place
the man's face as hard as you try to

Hey! Wake up, niggers! Or we all through!

The pitfalls of technology are examined here, and we see everything to be, in the way of technology (trick/knowledge) becoming the ultimate enemy. In mankind's mad quest to compete with the creator, they have transgressed all bounds. Thus mankind lives on the precipice of total annihilation because of what its own hands have wrought. In the 'Mean Machine' we see a flood of technology swamping the people. Under the guise of progress, the technology has stretched the limits of the imagination. The Jinni is slowly materializing from out of the lamp, and soon he will grant their death wish. A wolf in sheep's clothing, the 'Mean Machine' shows the selling of mankind's soul for the realm of a mechanized, electronic, atomic pseudo-paradise here on earth. Written in 1971, the 'Mean Machine' foresees how the machine turns mean and dominates the scene. Recently a verse from the poem came to pass. The verse was: 'Radar, sonar laser beams, jets, tanks, submarines, megatons, H-bomb, napalm, gas! All this shit will kill you fast'. A Russian jet shot down KLM Flight 007. Napalm was used in Vietnam, and gas was used (accidentally of course) in Bhopal, India, bringing the death toll to 2,500 and rising. Recently re-recorded by myself and Grandmixer D.S.T., the 'Mean Machine' was put out as a 12-inch single. This is my way of saying: Warning – the Tricknology will Cur-ill You!

Driving me **nuts,** bolts, screws
I got the blues from paying dues
for programmed news of honeycoated lies
Your eyes can't believe
That weave the Devil's magic with the latest gadget
from the Mean Machine
A'running the Same Game with Another Name
Down to your brain, blowing your mind
Stealing your time, smooth and slick
with the latest trick to get rich quick
from nonsense at your mind's expense
as your mind digs the scene

from the Mean Machine
designed to drive your brain insane
Loudspeakers blasting inside your head
saying what someone else said
for you to do what they want you to
No. Go. Fast. Slow
Getting you high off the latest lie
Telling you when, where, how and why
as your mind digs the scene
from the Mean Machine,
A'running the Same Game with Another Name
Factories of insanity playing on your vanity
as they distort your sense of self
Telling you what you need and how to succeed
as they steal all of your wealth
Probing your mind, trying to find
how to scheme on you best
From programmed schools with Devilish rules
putting you to the test
Death dealing devices sold at high prices
designed with you in mind to buy
as they kill you slow and some of y'all don't even know
y'all paying the Machine to die
Mechanized lies dressed up in disguise
in forms of various kinds
Treachery and deceit the people must defeat
in the battle for free men's minds
For complete domination is the goal of this nation
of all free thinking thought
and those who oppose will be killed by their foes
the flunkies whose souls have been bought
Transplants to revive the living dead
replacing the truth with lies instead
Newspapers, radios, TVs

spreading lies across seven seas
Robot men with computers for brains
Space ships, cars, trains and planes
All calculated to blow your mind
Moving faster than your sense of time
Living luxuriously soft while the people slave hard
For the Devil would have you believe he is God
Chemical drugs that keep you high
while the Mean Machine creates another lie
for power and glory and world wide fame
while Running the Same Game with Another Name
It's the computer's equation for world wide invasion
that comes in the name of peace and goodwill
But all of them are lying as they keep on trying
to set the people up for the kill
Population control of the people with soul
all over the planet Earth.
Manipulating their will with a tiny white pill
to control their natural birth
Behind the scene schemes furthering the Mean Machine's dreams
of conquest and world domination
from the farthest depths of the universe
to the smallest earthly nation

Radar, Sonar, Laser beams!
Jets, Tanks, Submarines!
Megathons, H-Bombs, Napalm, Gas!

All this shit will kill you fast
All products of the Mean Machine
The Devil disguised as a human being
And he will even preach that God is dead
And some of y'all will believe what the Devil has said
And he will then act as the world's police
And the sun will rise up in the West

and set down in the East

And when it came time for the end...
And when it came time for the end...
And when it came time for the end...
The men will look like the women
and the women like the men
And some will dance in a hypnotic trance
like as if they have no care
But these will be signs of the changing times
that the end is drawing near
For it was prophesized many centuries past
that the end will come in a fiery holocaust
and only the righteous people will survive the blast
and the Devil's machine will bring about his own end
and peace, love and joy will reign once again

and man will understand man
and man will understand man
and man will understand man
and man will understand man
and man will understand man
and man will understand man
and live in harmony and peace
and the sun will once again
rise up in the East

BIRD'S WORD

A tribute to the masters of the art form known as jazz. A mini epic of approximately eighty-four blues/jazz singers and musicians. In a kaleidoscope of spoagraphics we view a mini mystery of evolution revealing the sequences of musical events taking place at a fast pace like a race in time and space (I don't mean to rhyme but it is on time). Twisting, turning, twirling, swirling, like gold or sterling, moving, grooving, proving that the rhythm is rooted to the soil/soul. Named after the impeccable, irrepressible 'Yardbird' aka Charlie Parker. 'Bird's Word' is the poem of a bird whom Bird is named after. (To any that I might have left out, I extend my personal apologies, as it was due to my fallibility as a member of the created human beings. As a consolation it is my pleasure to inform you that the creator has given you this talent, and he will suffice you.) 'Bird's Word' is self-evident, a testimony to itself. Building at will, a moving picture still, a swing thing on a riff, a divine gift, a downward-up lift, a consolation prize, still on the rise, it flows, glows and shows... The word is be-bop non-stop.

Everything was silent
and then Ma Rainey spread *Black News*
by way of the *Backwater Blues*
as Bessie Smith picked up on it

and spread the word, thru music and song,
then the message passed on
to Chick Webb, King Oliver, Buddy Bolden and Jelly Roll Morton,
and they played the word and passed it along to Louis Armstrong
Fats Navarro, Charlie Ventura, Roy Eldridge and Fats Waller,
who was known to holler
The joint is jumpin with a Fatman's joy
as everybody started *Stompin' at the Savoy*
Then the word grew strong, as the immortal *Bird* came along
and blew all the Blackness that was true
with some Be-Bop brand new
turning everybody on, with his unforgettable horn
as Lester Young became the first *Prez* of our race
and we turned around and dug on the beautiful face of Billie Holiday
As Billie began to sing praises to the blackman's thing,
the good Brother Monk threw in some funk
so that the whole world could see
what he is, was and always will be
A genius creatively!
Then Miles began to set new styles
that put us miles ahead,
as Dizzy set us free to be ourselves,
and ride to heaven from hell in the latest
El-Do-Ra-Do, comin' for to carry us home!
Then Dinah sang finer
As Duke and Ella rode to fame
goin' to Harlem on the *A train*
and we tuned into Charlie Mingus's bass
setting a soulful pace
that let us taste the down sound,
that found our hearts beating to the voice and drums
of Abbey Lincoln and Max Roach
in their hip approach to Blackness!
Then Eddie Jefferson crooned an original tune
as Lambert, Hendricks and Ross scatted a new course

and we sampled King Pleasure's treasure
and listened to James Moody's moans
and then dug the dynamite drums of Brother Phily Joe Jones!
As Milt Jackson played the vibes in leaps and strides
with the MJQ
that sped our prides into sophisticate funkiness
Meanwhile, Sonny Rollins was building a bridge,
for us to leave behind our grief
for the soulful relief
to find our own black minds
to tune in on Bud Powell
who played the piano with funky hands
as he filled the seats and made 'em stand
on funky nights down *Birdland*
Then the Mighty Hawk made his horn talk
and we heard Baby Ray play *What'd I say*
and jammed the set to dig Ornette
as Art Blakey broke free
spreadin' the message to you and me
to dig on the trumpet of *KD*
as we broadened our range
and counted our change with Basie
As Earl *Fatha* Hines blew our minds
and we grew fonder of Errol Garner
as Eddie Harris bent our ear talkin' bout *Listen Here*
and Eric Dolphy made his stand
with a side called *Ironman*
and Gene Ammons told his soul
and we mined Horace's Silver
that bought funky gold
Then Oscar Brown and Joe Williams got down
and we spun around, spun around, spun around, spun around, spun
    around, spun around, spun around, spun around, spun around, spun
        around, spun around, spun around, spun around, spun around
            and dug Clifford Brown,

blowin' a sweet funky sound of soul
with a rhythm of gold
and along, and along, and along, and along, and along, and along,
and along, and along, and along, and along, and along, and along,
and along, and along, and along, and along, and along,
and along **came 'trane!**
Who blew away all the pain, all the pain, all the pain, all the pain, all the
pain, all the pain, all the pain, all the pain, all the pain, all the pain
in the name of all the Black People on the Planet Earth,
and all the stars in the cosmic universe!
As Brother 'trane blew to the East
to destroy the beast
and bring back Peace to Black People!
And everybody heard the majestic word of 'trane's horn,
telling us of a *Love Supreme* for Black People,
that grew strong, and on, and on, and on, and on, and on, and on,
and on, and on, and on, and on, and on, and on, and on, and on,
and on, and on, and on, and on, and on, and on, and on,
from the soul, from the heart
from the spirit, from the brain
from the love of Brother John Coltrane!
Then Jimmy Smith got funky with it
and preached a sermon not to *Walk on the Wild Side*
but ride with Wes Montgomery
who played his best everyday in our life
as Shirley Scott's organ got hot
and she and Stanley set more funk free!
as Ahmed Jamal played with renewed ability
to give our minds some *Tranquillity*
so that we could listen to an in-soul depth
Brother Archie Shepp
as Jackie McClean broke on the scene
blowing mean and harder
for everybody to listen to Betty Carter

as Sun Ra shined
and Cannonball's horn whined

Mercy! Mercy! Mercy!

So Sonny Stitt started piping it
and we couldn't get enough of brother Jack McDuff
as Freddie Hubbard began to bud
and we heard from Donald Byrd
and they'll be no others like the Ayler Brothers
Then Wayne Shorter grew taller
and our ship left dock with Herbie Hancock
as we rolled with Lee Morgan
and *Grooved* on Richard Holmes' organ
and then dug the soul of Art Tatum
produce the sound that made him
as Rufus Harley blew an old new type bagpipe
that put the pants back on the man
an' Nina Simone groaned *Mississippi Goddam*!
and Brother McCoy gave us peace and joy
as Elvin bought our freedom *Jones* down on us!
Then Charles Lloyd filled the void
an' we watched Roland Kirk work!
and with a sigh of relief listened to Yusef Lateef
blow in a flow of flurry's of peace from the east
as Pharaoh Saunders floated down the Nile with Brother Leon Thomas
to herald the promise of peace and happiness throughout the land!
All praises due to the Creator of the **Blackman!**

Blackman!

'Opposites' is an attempt at reversing the negative thinking, an in-feriority complex from the legacy of slavery imposed on blacks by white race supremacists.

Understand, said the old black man
that everything works in opposites
The sun and the moon, left and right
Hot and cold, black and white
Understand, said the old black man
who is the opposite of you
Understand
so that you will know what you have to do
Understand
that black is true and false is white
Understand
that black is right and white is wrong
Understand
that white is weak and black is strong
Understand
that white is suffocation and black is a deep breath
Understand
that black is life and white is death
Understand
that blacks will live in glory while whites will die in shame
Understand
that blackness is reality and whiteness but a game
Understand
that blacks were here first and will be here last
Understand
that whitey steals your future and lies about your past
Understand
that before we were sold as slaves
the black man walked in temples of glory

while the white man crawled in caves
So understand, young black man
who is the opposite of you
Understand
so that you will know what you have to do
Understand
that black is the beginning of white's end
Understand
that whiteness is your enemy and blackness is your friend
Understand
the height and weight of your mental depth
Understand
that you're the original man as quiet as it's kept
Understand
that blacks will rise and whites will fall
Understand
that white equals nothing and black equals all
Understand
that our climate is hot and theirs is cold
And you are young and I am old
But all lies die when the truth is told
So understand, young black man
who is the opposite of you
Understand
so that you will know what you have to do
Understand
that black is love and white is hate
Understand
why our freedom cannot wait
Understand
that white is war and black is peace
Understand
that black is beauty and white the beast
Understand
that black is happiness and white is sorrow

Understand that I was a slave yesterday
But you'll be free tomorrow
And the second after **Before**
The minute after **Before**
The hour after **Before**
The day after **Before**
The week after **Before**
The month after **Before**
The year after **Before**
The decade after **Before**
The century after **Before**
The eternity after **Before**
you understand what it means to be a free **black** man

E PLURIBUS UNUM

Six months of research went into the writing of 'E Pluribus Unum'. The Latin had to be translated, and the symbology on the 'Great Seal' had to be interpreted. The conclusions were astounding to say the least, and shed much light on the intentions of the so-called Founding Fathers whose idea was to build a new Roman Empire. Thus one finds many of the public buildings in the U.S. are based on the Greco-Roman concepts of architecture. Thru our spoagraphic binoculars we re-rexamine the historical context of the grand Masonic plan, and why this seal was printed on the national currency. The institution of secret economics (ie hoarding) plays the most vital role in the 'spell' cast on the dollar bill, which in turn hypnotized the working masses 'in thinking paper money was real'. In fact the gold in Fort Knox is not par equivalent with the amount of paper money in circulation. Broken down further, we have 'doll' (ie facsimile), 'ar' (they ar unreal) B-ill (be-sick, out of balance, diseased - ill at ease) and so two economies emerge out of the 'eagle's claws, one peace time and one war time, the eagle being the national wildlife symbol. The number 'thirteen' is the key in this astrological/numerological, masonic/satanic spell. The evil eye of 'Nimrod' who built the Tower of Babel and ended up a babbling idiot, trying to defy the lords of the universe, (Rabbil-Alamin). He hangs over the pyramid as the capstone, bewitching all who watch, and causing the money to be 'the root of all evil'. Hence the dollar is referred to jokingly in the States as the Almighty Dollar, one of God's attributes (Al-Aziz).

56   Selfish desires are burning like fires
      among those who hoard the gold
      As they continue to keep the people asleep
      and the truth from being told
      Racism and greed keep the people in need
      from getting what's rightfully theirs
      Cheating, stealing and double-dealing
      as they exploit the people's fears
      Now, Dow Jones owns the people's homes
      and all the surrounding land
      Buying and selling their humble dwelling
      in the name of the Master Plan
      'Cause paper money is like a bee without honey
      with no stinger to back him up
      and those who stole the people's gold
      are definitely corrupt
      Credit cards, master charge, legacies of wills
      real-estate, stocks and bonds on coupon paper bills
      Now the US mints, on paper prints, millions every day
      and use the eagle for their symbol, cause it's a bird of prey
      The laurels of peace and the arrows of wars
      are clutched very tightly in the eagle's claws
      filled with greed and lust,
      and on the back of the dollar bill,
      is the words In God We Trust
      But the dollar bill is their only God
      and they don't even trust each other
      for a few dollars more they'd start a war
      to exploit some brother's mother
      Then there's the pyramid, that stands by itself
      created by a black people's knowledge and wealth
      and over the pyramid hangs the devil's eye
      that stole from the truth and created the lie
      Now annuit means an endless amount stolen over the years
      and coeptis means a new empire of vampire millionaires

And novus is a Latin word meaning something new
an ordo means a way of life chosen by a few
seclorum is a word that means to take from another
knowledge, wisdom and understanding stolen from the brother
Roman numerals on the base of the pyramid's face
tell the date they began to exist,
when they established this branch of hell
in seventeen-seventy-six
Now there are thirteen layers of stone on the pyramid alone
an unfinished work of art

for thirty-three and a third is as high as a mason can go
without falling apart
Thirteen stars in the original flag!
Thirteen demons from the Devil's bag!
Thirteen berries and thirteen leaves!
Thirteen colonies of land-grabbing thieves!
Thirteen arrows in the eagle's claws!
Sixty-seven corporations wage the Devil's wars!
Thirteen stripes on the eagle's shield!
And these are the symbols on the U.S. seal!
Now on the front of the dollar bill
to the right of Washington's head
is a small seal in the shape of a wheel
with the secret that's been left unsaid
The symbols in the middle represent the riddle
of the scales, the ruler and the key;
the square rule is a symbol
from the craft of masonry
The scales represent Libra
the balance of the seventh sign
They also represent the just-us
which you and I know is blind
The key unlocks the mysteries
of the secrets of the seal
So that only the Govern-u-men
would know what they reveal
The four words above form the last parts of
the secrets of the seal
and tells how they fooled the people
into thinking paper money was real!
Now, Thesaur means the treasury
where they store the gold they stole
and Amer means to punish
like the slaves they bought and stole
Then septent means seven

like seventeen-seventy-six
when the thirteen devils gathered
to unleash their bag of tricks
Then sigel means the images
they've created to fool the world
like the colours on Old Glory
the flag that they unfurled
Now red was the colour of the Indian man
White was the Jinns who stole the land
Blue was the eyes that hypnotised

with the tricks and traps they sprung
and even to this very same day
they all speak with forked tongue!
And so the power is in the hands of the ruling classes
playing god with the faith of all the masses
so the people don't get any in the land of the plenty
because E Pluribus Unum means One Out of Many!

WOODSHED WALK

Though I wander thru the woods on a lonesome trail
do you think I can't begin to think or even see?
the real, the re-al, the reality
You're out of your mind!
I went strolling down the woods the other day
trying hard to find out what it was I really wanted to play
The people thought that I would never play again
you see they really felt that I had peaked
and was on my way to a steady downward trend.
But I went right back into the woodshed
where I could try to free the self in me
and get deeper inside my head
My head, my head was talking while I went
walking down the trail
I came upon the shed, sitting way out there in the clearing
beckoning to my soul to play the things that I kept on hearing
It seemed to say come and play
come and play here in me
and I will really do my darndest
to try and help you to be free-e-e-e
If free is really what you wanna be now
then step inside of me
I stepped into the darkness
into the pitch black-black-black darkness
of lightly taking my axe right out of my case,
while ordering my foot to keep a steady even pace
Then I began to blow
Now-de-dum-tum-tum-tum-diddly-oop-en-oppen-ou-wee
you and me, were castaways on a sea
You and me were living our destiny...
Were riding the crest of the waves
up underneath the stars

62 **Do you think that this state will continue to exist?**
    Well you're wrong
    It won't be long before it's too late...
    You're out of your mind!

POEMS BY SULIAMAN EL HADI

IT'S A TRIP

How I wish I could stay, far away, far away
Away from the milling masses
Filth, vermin and gases
Muggings, thuggings, near naked bodies as they go marching past
Shamming at modesty in miniskirt mask
And it's a trip
Yes, it's a trip
From the screaming and cussin'
From the gambling and hustlin'
From the nodding and the fussin'
From the confusion of integration and segregation
amidst the cries of Let's build a nation!
Separation, y'all, separation, y'all
Separation, separation
It's a trip
Yes, I trip to escape the environmental rape
The industrial waste in the rivers and lakes
The mad, mad race for the vastness of space
The clamour and fuss to quicken the pace
The hypocrites' call of justice for all
though this cannot be for people like me
There's no place for the poor y'all, in this society
So I trip and I flee from the things that I see
Yes I trip and I flee from this brand of liberty
Yes I trip and I flee, so perhaps for a moment
I might be free, free, free
I might be free, free, free
And it's a trip
Yes, it's a trip
Yes, I split with my mind, through the passage of time
Back when men were still men, and the sisters were fine
And a man had a friend, and a man had Allah

And a man had some land, and a faith to defend
Back in time before men were deceived by the Jinn
Back in time before men were deceived by the Jinn
But, alas, I come back to the real, to the fact
Being poor, being black, being under attack
Being under attack for just being black
Being under attack for just being black
Being under attack for just being black
Being under attack and that is a fact
And it's a trip
It's a trip
Yes, it's time we all took a real hard look
at the lifestyles we have and the ones we foresook
And our past and our present, at the future we crave
And at the things we encounter between the womb and the grave
And what we must do, and what must be saved
And how we must struggle, and how things will be
when truth is revealed, y'all, and falsehood has died
And we can be free and we want to be
And it's a trip
And it's a trip
How I wish I could stay, far away, far away
From the witches and vampires that stalk me each day
Far away from the hunter that makes me the prey
Far away from the snare that they lay on the way
For the soul is the prize in the game that they play
For the soul is the prize in the game that they play!

HO CHI MINH

He stood
and looked upon the earth
his weapons in his hand
His eyesight came to rest
upon an **ancient** little man
Tilling the soil and casting nets
his flock and herds to tend
yet ready at a moment's call
his homeland to defend
He walked into the other's land
an uninvited guest
He said I'm here to rid you of
a **menace** and a **pest**
He said I'll build an army base

70 right here upon your shores
And I'll protect you from your sons
and from the guy next door
The old man answered with a snap
I need no help from you
Why, you're the same one that I fought
at Diem Bien Phu
My sons are out upon the fields
their country to regain
So why don't you just go back home
and save us both some pain?

He said Old man, are you insane?
Do you know who I am?
Why, I'm the policeman of the world
and they call me Uncle Sam
The old man took his weapon up
and with a real defiant stand
he said *Yes, I know you and what you'll do*
But you see, I just don't give a damn
He said Where did this little man
get the audacity
to take a weapon in his hand
and speak like that to me?
I'll send my helicopters out
to hunt the peasant down
I'll send my jets and my tanks
to burn his villages to the ground
The old man looked up at this fool
and did not even bat an eye
He said *Before we would submit*
you see, we all would rather die
But I feel it fair
that I should warn you for your sake
This here will be the biggest blunder

*that you'll **ever** make*

The bully, now blushing red
let out a battle cry
The old man just seemed to fade away
into the countryside
He smiled and said with confidence
I've got him on the run
But poonji sticks and booby traps
set fire to his buns
The old man fought so hard and well
that so the story goes
he trapped him, a paper tiger
and filled his hide with holes
And as the pain intensified
he cried out loud and clear
If I could just get untangled, y'all
I'm gettin' on out of here
You see, I just could not win
against Ho Chi Minh
No, I just could not win
against Ho Chi Minh

Blessed are those who struggle
Oppression is worse than the grave
Better to die for a noble cause
than to live and die a slave

Blessed are those who courted death
Who offered their lives to give
Who dared to rebel, rather than serve
to die so that we might live

Blessed are those who took up arms
and dared to face our foes
Nat Turner, Vesey, Gariel, Chinque
To mention a few names we know

Blessed are the memories of those who were there
at the Harper's Ferry Raid
Strong were their hearts, noble their cause
and great was the price they paid

Blessed are the voices of those who stood up
and cried out, *Let us be free!*
Douglas and Garvey and Sojourner Truth
Dubois and Drew Ali

Blessed are the giants that we have loved
and lost to the bullet's sting
like Malcolm and Medgar and the Panthers who fell
and Martin Luther King

And blessed are the bodies of those who were hung
from the limbs of the sycamore tree
Who found end to their hope at the end of a rope
'cause they dared to attempt to be free

Up through the years we've continued this fight

our liberty to attain
And though we have faced insurmountable odds
yet the will to resist remains

Blessed are the spirits of those who have died
in the prisons all over this land
who committed one sin, they stood up like men
and got iced for just being a man

Blessed all you who will join with us now
in this struggle of life and death
so that freedom and peace will be more than a word
to the offspring that we have left

Are you aware of the pill?
Its basic design is to kill
The fertile womb
becomes a tomb
for a new child unborn still

I say, are you aware of the brute
whose job is to wither the fruit?
They'll cause us to fall
our history and all
by cuttin' us off at the root

They say We'll stunt Africa's growth
And Asia has too many folks
Too large is the mouth
in the Latin South
We'll aid 'em by cuttin' their throats

No, we must approach as a friend
and do our job from within
We'll feed 'em the pill
that's made up to kill
and make their beginning their end

So poor folks of the world be aware
For their evil design is laid bare
Watch out for the hag
with the little black bag
marked Birth Control Peace Corps and Care

It's part of a game that they play
And it's designed to make poor people pay
It's part of a lie
to help you to die
while they cart your resources away

I say conspiracy is in the air
to control the children you bear
Control of the land
is a part of the plan
as your kind grows increasingly rare

It's a truth to be understood
though at first it may appear good
But it's a menace to health
and to lineal wealth
since you can't reproduce when you should

And in this respect I am told
it is better to use self-control
For the future and truth
belongs to the youth
since you cannot prevent growing old

So make sure that your reasoning is sound
before taking that love potion down
For it would be a shame
to come into fame
for being the last one around

Stream in which I bathe my face
help me soar above this place
Leave me not to wander
Leave me not to wander

Stream in which I bathe my face
help me soar above this place
Leave me not to wander
Leave me not to wander

Stream in which I bathe my face
help me soar above this place
Leave me not to wander
Leave me not to wander

Stream in which I bathe my face
Help me soar above this place
Leave me not to wander
in disgrace, in disgrace

Reason draws itself the line
El Quran the signs define
Let me taste the vintage
of the vine, divine

Help my feet to enter in
where the garden streams begin
Save me from the consequence
of sin, within

Sit me down on thick brocade
served by youth who never age
basking in the shade
that never fades

Guide me past that fiery room
where the inmates that are doomed
sit waiting
midst the stench and gloom

Midst the crying and regret
standing ankle deep in sweat
vibing on a threat
that came too soon

Stream in which I bathe my face
help me soar above this place
Leave me not to wander
Leave me not to wander

Stream in which I bathe my face
help me soar above this place
Leave me not to wander
in disgrace, in disgrace

In the shadow of the throne
is where I want to make my home
Boundless stores of mercy
there are known, and shown

All the good one could acquire
Large eyed virgins with pure desire
Help me to retire
beyond the fire

Just watch my mortal soul take flight
and gift me with a sharper sight
Spur me to ascend the higher heights
of light

Here is where I want to be
where my soul is burden free
Bathin' in a sea of tranquility
That's for me

Stream in which I bathe my face
help me soar above this place
Leave me not to wander
Leave me not to wander

Stream in which I bathe my face
help me soar above this place
Leave me not to wander
in disgrace, in disgrace

Clothed in robes of gold and silk
lofty mansions custom built
enchanted springs of honey
and of milk

Surround myself with treasures rare
Peace notes saturate the air
Rewarded for past actions
that my soul did bear

Song my truer self doth sing
Peace and joy about me ring
Glory to my Lord
the King of Kings

Stream in which I bathe my face
help me soar above this place
Leave me not to wander
in disgrace, in disgrace

Stream in which I bathe my face
help me soar above this place
Leave me not to wander
Leave me not to wander

Stream in which I bathe my face
help me soar above this place
Leave me not to wander
in disgrace, in disgrace

In the shadow of the throne
is where I want to make my home
Boundless stores of mercy
there are known and shown

All the good one could acquire
Large eyed virgins with pure desire
Help me to retire
beyond the fire

OH MY PEOPLE

The happy-go-lucky attitude of our people in the midst of adversity served as the basis for the writing of this poem. Here we call upon them to stop, be still, and subject themselves to self scrutiny, and after identifying their weaknesses, correct them. As was said in the past by the prophet of God Almighty, peace upon him, 'God will not change the condition of a people until they first change themselves'.

Oh my people, what is your worth?
What is your worth, what is your worth, child of the earth?
Are you like silver, diamonds or gold
increasing in value as you grow old?
Or are you like dew at the start of the day
like smoke in the wind, slowly fading away?
You cannot be measured in dollars or cents
You can only be measured in your deeds and intent
And what you achieve and how you relate
And what are your virtues and if you are great
Why you are here in this degraded old state
A victim of scorn, contempt and of hate?
Why can't your hearts be united as one

for a cause such as freedom for the future to come?
What kind of veils hide your eyes from the truth
why do you not research and establish the proof
of where you have come from and what was your way?
Let us find some solutions for the moral decay
that frightens our elders and shatters our homes
abandoning our offspring to a fate of their own
We must rise up, my people, from the depth of our dust
To a new understanding built on mutual trust
To some solid achievements and a new way of life
bringing end to the conflicts and eternal strife
that plagues our existence and threatens our end
We must define our enemy and just who is our friend
And then, my people, and only then
can we raise up our heads among the nations of men
Reclaiming our birth right, reasserting our pride
reuniting our families, increasing our stride
New rules of our choosing, new goals to attain
One god, one destiny one people, one aim
And oh my people, what a wonderful day
when we use our talent in a positive way
Providing ourselves with the things that we need
Purging our systems of envy and greed
Reshaping our image, emerging as one
setting righteous examples for the children to come
Then maybe, my people, just maybe you'll find
some joy that's been hidden in your space in time
And in your assent you will find that it's true
there is no treasure more precious than you
Oh my people, what is your worth
What is your worth, what is your worth, child of the earth?

'Hands Off' is a protest against racism. It tells Western society to examine its roots and take stock of the contributions that black people have made to the development of the West. It points out the Moors and their African roots and what they accomplished in Spain, Portugal and Italy. Their contributions to medicine and the other sciences. It also reminds the West of the important role the African slaves played in the building of the North and South of the American continent.

Tell me not that I'm a dreamer for the things I feel and see
or that nothing can be accomplished from the things I wish to be
Tell me not that I'm fanatic for the things I feel inside
they are flowers of oppression born of a pain I cannot hide
Do not look upon my actions as the acts of one insane
when I take up modern weapons to avenge my father's name
Let your eyes scan on the Ghettos, through the books of history
then you'll understand this feeling and just how it came to be
Sure I must admit I'm bitter for the precious blood I've bled
and for the years of cruel oppression that you've heaped upon my head
For the rape of my grandmothers and the mulattos that you've left
for the many, many, many, many, many, many, many, many, many, many,
many, many, **many** years of slavery with its legacy of death
Tell me not that I'm a dreamer, oh no it's **you** that cannot see
I am just another victim of a cruel reality
What manner of man is this, I ask? Who roams the seven seas
who graces the skies of birds of iron and wanders where he please
Who walks into another's home and **takes** his property
Then **slays** the man, his wife **and** child in the name of liberty
What manner of beast is this I ask who drops a napalm from the skies
then send **my** sons away to war to maim and kill and die
What manner of man is this I ask, who arrogantly displays his might
What manner of man is this, my friend, needless to say he's white
So take your hands off of me, white folks, I've done you no wrong
I'm only guilty of making you strong

I've built all of your cities and I've worked in your mines
I've fought to protect you many a time
It was I who taught you what it is to be brave
I had great civilizations when you lived in caves
I taught you what soap was when you dyed yourselves blue
I taught you of planting and harvesting too
I showed you what clothes were to cover your backs
when you were wearing wolfskins and running in packs
When you knew nothing of the barrier of sound
It was I who taught you that this planet was round
In Palermo, Sicily and Italy and Spain
I left monuments of my grandeur and fame
And during your dark ages when your people were blind
I built universities to enlighten your kind
When your homeland was weak and your people were poor
It was I who brought you to America's shore
Why you did not even know how to survive
I showed you medicine to keep you alive
How earnest you seem, how well you did learn
how vile a reward I received in return
But time is on my side, I'm sure you must know
that the day will arrive when you'll reap what you sow
For I gave you Religion and you know it's a fact
that the Christ **and** the Buddha **and** Mohammed were black
I taught you to dance and I taught you to sing
You repaid me with treachery and slavery and chains
So don't touch me Whitey and don't look surprised
No I'm no longer fooled by your tricks and your lies
I'm aware of your game and of your history
and I'm aware of the Judas that you've been to me
So watch out for me white folks, it's just a matter of time
I'll soon be together, then Vengeance is mine

A historical portrait of America before the European occupation. Emphasis is laid on the richness of the original culture, the vastness of the territory and abundance of the natural resources. It was inspired by the injustices and lack of sensitivity shown by the government towards the native Americans. If one sees evil, he should stop it by his hands. If he is unable, then at least he should speak out against it. If he can't do even that, then he should hate it in his heart - that is the lowest form of faith.

Happy the days when once we roamed
the land completely free
Good were the times when Village Heads
dictated policy.
Great was the hunting in those days
abundant was the game
Peaceful relations we all had
Before the white man came

Tall was the stalks of corn we grew
Large, the tobacco leaf
Healthy our bodies and our minds
Strong were our backs and teeth
Many a moonlit night was spent
dancing around the flame
Never a hungry moment met
Before the white man came

Clear were the streams that cross this place
Fishing was at its best
Silver and Gold the trinkets we wore
In the finest of clothes we were dressed
Large were the herds of long horn steer
and buffalo on the plains
Full was the peace-pipe that we smoked
Before the white man came

86   And then the day of the curse arrived
      and they landed on these shores
      What manner of being is this? we said
      We've never seen them before
      But even so we extended them our hand
      As we would unto a friend
      How could we have known that syphillis
      and claps and plague had come with them

      And now it's been 400 years
      since that eventful day
      but if we had known what they had in mind
      They would all have died in the bay
      So now we are paying for our mistake
      with only ourselves to blame
      With memories of the good old years
      Before the white man came.

THIS IS YOUR LIFE

A capsule view of the arms race and colonization of space. The development of robot technology and the subsequent threat to human society as we know it. It warns of the impending nuclear holocaust that hangs over the heads of all of humankind and exposes the greedy motives of those who would hold us all hostage for wealth and power.

You have nothing to say, just hear and obey
just silently playing your roles
while others decide whether you live or die
and madmen man the controls

It's a quarter to the hour and the superpowers
are standing toe to toe
They are talking slick and moving quick
and the whole thing's about to blow

They are acting tough and calling our bluff
while human masses cringe in fear
Knowing one mistake could seal their fate
and they might not see another year
They are viewing the world like a giant pearl
to be split down the middle
but the ultimate goal is total control
and that presents a riddle
It's beneath the ground that treasures are found
and humanity is in the way
So all the rest are pawns at best
in this deadly game of chess they play

They are in a race to conquer space
and build an artificial planet
but will the prize be our demise
for taking things for granted?
They ought to be alarmed at the nuclear arms
that they are putting into place
We've got to save our behinds by using our minds
and staying on the case
There'll be no time to dash when you see the flash
It's gonna come all of a sudden
So just close your eyes and realize
that some fool done pushed the button
And that mushroom cloud hangin' like a shroud
and the atmosphere all a-flame
Not even time to pray on this awful day
and nobody left to blame
There'll be no property harm with the neutron bomb
not very much devastation
but what worries me is if there'll be
any future generation
So tell me, why stand idly by
lost in song and laughter?

When the next day you see in reality
just might be the morning after

You have nothing to say, just hear and obey
just silently playing your roles
While others decide whether you live or die
and madmen man the controls

They could at least make a bid for peace
before they get down to the wire
They could avoid a fight, reduce military might
if peace is what they desire
But if they don't try, why we all must die
along with the earth
and if that's the deal, let's be for real
what would it all be worth?
The trillions they waste on developing space
could be better spent on the poor
We have plenty to give and we deserve to live
like the generations gone before
So what's it going to be for you and for me
when robots are ruling the land
And the latest craze will be to slave
for some computerized superman
It's part of a dream, a diabolical scheme
to develop a mechanical race
Hatching robot babes from mechanical eggs
and designing them to take our place
So we'd better not wait until it's too late
to try and stop this final war
'cause if we don't succeed there will be no need
since we won't exist anymore
So don't be deceived and please don't believe
you can survive a nuclear blast
because once it hits, why then, that's it
you are something of the past

90

And in some distant clime, in some distant time
from some other galaxy
They will survey the poles of the gaping hole
where this planet used to be
So that's the threat, the stage is set
the countdown has begun
Maybe we'll see the benefits
in some future life to come

'Get Moving' is a call to rising from apathy, from ignorance, from incompetence, from fear, from silent suffering to action, reform, development, to self confidence, self esteem, to self support and self dependence, to cultural, social, political and economic independence.

What you gonna do
you better get moving before we all are through
What you gonna do
you better get moving before we all are through

Wake up mighty nation from your sleep
Flex your muscles, stand up on your feet
Put your fears behind and activate your mind
Know that the taste of freedom is bitter sweet
Speak up loudly, let your voice be heard
Train your tongue to speak the righteous word
Think before you talk and look before you walk
To be oppressed forever, why that's absurd!
Come on, do your part before you die
Don't let a chance for freedom pass you by
You owe it to the youth, to search and find the truth
Results depend on just how hard you try
You must look to the future right away
You must get on the move without delay
And when all is said and done and victory is won
you will find you've moved the obstacles away
Wake up yourself from this unpleasant dream
Your limbs must work together as a team
Your future could be great if you cooperate
Believe me things ain't always what they seem

Break the bonds that hold you to the earth
Free yourself, show the world your worth
Let your motto be *I'm determined to be free*

To give my children freedom from the birth
Unleash that talent, put your mind to work
Who knows what joys behind tomorrow lurks
It's time to take a stand and give yourself a hand
But first you must be free of doubt and shirk
Search your soul, free yourself within
Let the truth become your bosom friend
Make your motives right and your future could be bright
Just reassure youself that you can win
Put your words and actions in accord
Keep your obligations to your Lord
The time is much too late to procrastinate
Your actions will determine your reward
Wake up, wake up, I've got to say it twice
It ain't nothing happening without some sacrifice
So do what you got to do, before we all are through
If you want freedom, prepare to pay the price

What you gonna do
you better get moving before we all are through!
What you gonna do
you better get moving before we all are through!